Geruafe

Markham

THE COMPLEAT HORSEMAN

THE COMPLEAT
HORSEMAN

BY

GERVASE MARKHAM

Author of A Discourse of Horsemanship,
Cavelarice or The English Horse-
man, Markham's Faithfull
Farrier, The Perfect
Horseman.

Edited by DAN LUCID *with pictures by*
PAULINE BAYNES. *Made and sold
by Houghton Mifflin Company
of Boston under the sign
of the Boy and His
Dolphin.*

MCMLXXV

This book is adapted from *Cheape and Good Husbandry*,
published by Gervase Markham in 1614, reissued in 1616, and
included in *A Way to get Wealth*, 15 editions, 1623–1695.

Library of Congress Cataloging in Publication Data

Markham, Gervase, 1568?–1637.
  The compleat horseman.

  Excerpted from various editions of the author's
Cheape and good husbandry, first published in 1614.
    1. Horsemanship—Early works to 1800.   2. Horses—
Early works to 1800.   I. Lucid, Dan.   II. Title.
SF309.M362 1975   636.1'08   75–8544
ISBN 0–395–21499–8

Printed in the United States of America

OO   10   9   8   7   6   5   4   3   2   1

For Mr. Bo Jangles

*The Horse will take such delight
and pleasure in his keeper's company, that he shall never approach
him but the horse will with a kind of
cheerful or inward neighing show
the joy he takes to behold him, and
where this mutual love is knit and
combined, there the beast must needs
prosper and the rider reap reputation
and profit.*

Gervase Markham

Contents

THE COMPLEAT HORSEMAN

Of the Horse in general

The Horse of all Creatures is the noblest, strongest, and aptest to do the best and worthiest services both in Peace and War. He is valiant, strong, and nimble, and above all other beasts most apt and able to endure the extremest labors. The moist quality of his composition is such that neither extreme heat doth dry up his strength nor the violence of cold freeze the warm temper of his moving spirits, and where there is any temperate government, there he withstandeth all effects of sickness with an uncontrolled constancy. He is most gentle and loving, apt to be taught and not forgetful when an impression is fixed in his brain. He is watchful above all other beasts, and will endure his labor with the most empty stomach. He is naturally given to much cleanliness, is of an excellent scent, and offended with nothing so much as evil smells.

CHAPTER ONE

Training the Horse

We shall now say something of the commendable exercise of riding great Horses. Our English Gentry from a sloth in their industry aim for the most part at no more skill than the riding of a ridden and perfect horse, which is but only the setting forth of another rider's virtue, and thereby making themselves richer in discourse than action. But the true Horse-rider shall not only recreate himself by riding the Horses whom others have made perfect, but shall by his own practice bring his Horse from utter ignorance to the best skill that can be desired in his motions. From this he shall find a twofold pleasure, the one an excellent contentment to his mind, that he can perform so worthy an action without the chargeable assistance of others, and the other a healthful support to his body, when by such recreation his spirits and inward faculties are revived and inflamed.

First then to speak of the taming of a young *The taming of a young Colt.*

15

Colt, which is as it were the preface or introduction to the art of Riding. You shall keep him in the house a week or fortnight until he is familiar with you and will withal patiently endure currying, combing, clawing and handling in every part and member of his body without any show of rebellion or knavishness, which you shall compass by all gentle and easy means, doing nothing about him suddenly or rashly, but with leisure and moderation.

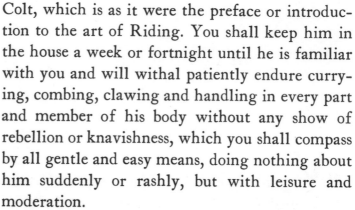

His saddling and bridling.

Then shall you offer him a Saddle, which you shall set in the manger before him that he may smell to it and look upon it, and you shall jingle the girths and stirrups about his ears to make him careless of the noise. Then with all gentleness, after you have rubbed his sides therewithal, you shall set the saddle on his back and gird it gently on, and then place his Crupper with all ease, which done, you shall take a sweet snaffle bit washed and anointed with honey and salt, and put it into his mouth. This you shall do in the morning as soon as you have groomed him, and then thus saddled and bridled, you shall lead him forth, and water him in your hand abroad.

When bringing him in, after he hath stood a little reined upon his bit an hour or more, take

away the bridle and saddle, and let him go to his
feed till the evening. In the evening, lead him
forth as before with his saddle to the water and
when he is set up, gently take off his saddle and
cherish him, then groom him and clothe him up
for the night.

The next day saddle and bridle him as before
said, and put on him a strong nose-band and
Martingale, which you shall buckle at such length
that he may no more but feel it when he jerketh
up his head, and then lead him forth into some
new plowed field or soft ground. There after you
have made him trot a good space about in your
hand, and thereby taken away from him all his
wantonness and knavish distractions, you shall
offer your foot to the stirrup. If he show any distaste either in body or countenance, you shall then
course him about again, then offer again, and with
leisure rise half way up, and go down again. If he
shrink, correct him as before, but if he take it
patiently, then cherish him and so mount into
the Saddle.

The first mounting.

After cherishing, light down again and give
him bread or grass to eat. Look that your Girths
be well girted and tight, that the Crupper be
strong and of just length, that the Bridle hang

17

even and in its due place, without inward or outward offence, that your stirrups be fit, and generally all things without offence to your self or to the beast. Then as before, mount his back, seat your self just and even in the Saddle, make the reins of your Bridle of equal length, carry your rod without offence to his eye in your right hand, the point either directly upright or thwarted towards your left shoulder.

Having cherished him, let the Groom lead him forward a dozen or twenty paces, then gently straining your hand, with the help of the Groom make him stand still, cherish him and lead him forward again. Do this five or six times one after another, till by continual use you make him of your own accord (without the Groom's help), by giving your body and thrusting your Legs forward, go forward. As soon as he doth, you shall stay him, cherish him, and bring him to the block, where, after you have cherished him, you shall gently alight, cause him to be set up, well groomed, and fed.

The next day you shall bring him forth as before, and in all points take his back as aforesaid, and so by the help of the Groom, trot forthright half a mile at the least. Then let the Groom lay off his hand and walk by him, till you have of your self trotted him forth another half mile. Cherish him and have the Groom give him some grass or bread to eat, and then trot him home and bring him back to the block as before, and there alight and so set him up.

The third day let your Groom light upon some fair Jade, and, bringing your Colt to the block, take his back gently, and after you have cherished him, the other riding before you, follow him forthright a mile. Ever and anon, at the end of twenty or thirty score, stop the colt gently, cherish him, and make him yield and go back a step or two, and then put him forward again, till he be so perfect that with the least motion he will go forward, stop and retire.

If the Colt chance at any time to strike or rebel, you shall make him which rides before you take the spare Rein and lead him forward, whilst you give him two or three good lashes under the belly, and then take the spare rein to your self again till all faults be amended.

Then you shall spare your Guide, and only by your self for three or four days more trot him at least a mile or two forward, using him only to stop or retire, and bringing him home a contrary

way to that you went forth, till he be so perfect and willing that he will take his way how or in what manner your self pleaseth. Always observe to mount and dismount at the block only, unless some special occasion constrain you to the contrary.

This you may very well bring to pass the first week of the Horse's riding.

The three main points of a Rider's skill: Helps, Corrections, Cherishings.

As soon as you see your Horse will receive you to his back, trot forthright, stop and retire, and do all this with great patience and obedience, you shall then call into your mind the three main points of a Rider's knowledge, which are helps, corrections, and cherishings.

For *Helps*, the first is the voice, which soundeth sharply and cheerfully, crying *via, how, hey*, and such like, adding a spirit and liveliness to the horse and lending a great help to all his motions. The second is the bridle, which restrained or at liberty shows him how and which way to go. Then the Rod, which being only shown, is a help to direct; being only moved, helps the quickness and nimbleness of the motion; and being gently touched withal, helps the loftiness of a Horse's jumps and leaps, and makes him as it were gather all his strength into one point. Lastly, the calves

20

of the legs, stirrup-Leathers and Stirrups, when moved by the horse's side, help him to nimbleness, swiftness and readiness in turning.

Some to these helps add the help of the Spur, but it must be done in a just and true time, and with such gentle bitterness that the Horse may understand it for a help. Otherwise he will take distaste, and finding it savor like of correction, so that instead of bettering his doings it will cause more disorders, such as sprawling with his fore-feet in advancing, jerking out with one or both his hinder feet in leaping or bounding, and shaking his head, and such like, as will appear in practise.

Now of *Corrections*, the most principal is the Spur, which must not at any time be given triflingly or itchingly, but soundly and sharply, as oft as just occasion shall require. The next is the Rod, which upon disorder, sloth or miscarriage of the members, must be given also soundly. Then there is the voice, which being delivered sharply and roughly, as *ha villain, carridro, diablo*, and such like threatenings, terrifieth the Horse and maketh him afraid to disobey. Lastly, there is the Bridle, which now and then stricken with a hard check in his mouth reformeth any vices

and distemperatures of his Head, but this last must be done seldom and with great discretion, for to make a Custom thereof is the ready way to spoil a Horse's Mouth.

Now of *Cherishings*, there are generally in use but three. First is the voice, which being delivered smoothly and lovingly, as crying *holla, so boy, there boy there*, and such like, gives the Horse both cheerfulness of Spirit and a knowledge that he hath done well. Then there is the hand, by clapping him gently on the Neck or Buttock, or giving him Grass or other Food to eat after he hath pleased you. Lastly there is the big end of the Rod, by rubbing him therewith upon the withers or mane, which is very pleasing and delightful to the Horse.

Of the Nose-Band and Martingale.

Now after these ordinary and usual helps, corrections, and cherishings, you shall have respect to the Nose-Band or Nose-Band and Martingale, which carry in them all the three former both several and united. It is first an especial help and guide to every well-disposed Horse for setting of his head in a true place, forming of his Rein, and making him appear comely and gallant in the Eyes of the beholders. Then it is a sharp correction when a Horse jerketh out his Nose or disordereth his head any way or striveth to plunge or run away with his Rider. And lastly, it is a great cherishing unto the Beast when he yieldeth his Head to your hand by shrinking from his Face and so leaving nothing more to torment him except when he offendeth. Whence it comes that more from this than any thing else, the Horse first gaineth the knowledge of his Master's Will and is desirous to perform it. Therefore you shall be very careful to the placing of this upon the Horse.

At first it should hang somewhat low and rest upon the tender Gristle of the Horse's Nose, whereby corrections may be the sharper when occasion requires it. Then it should be loose and not tight, whereby the Horse may feel upon the yielding of his Head how the offence goeth from him and so know that only his own disorder is his own punishment. Lastly, he shall be careful to note how he winneth the Horse's Head and by degrees to draw his Martingale tighter and tighter so as the horse may ever have a gentle feeling of the same, and no more, till his Head and Rein be brought to that perfection that you desire, and then there to stay. Keep the Martingale constantly in that place only, which you shall perform in

23

those few days which you trot your Horse forthright, before bringing him to any Lesson more than the knowledge of your self and how to receive you to his back and trot forth obediently with you.

Of treading the large Ring. When your Horse is brought unto some certainty of Rein, will trot forthright with you at your pleasure, and by your former exercise therein is brought to breath and delight in his travail, which will grow and increase upon him as you grow and increase in your labor, then you shall bring him to the treading forth of the large Rings.

If he be of heavy and sluggish nature, slothfull and dull, albeit he have strength and sufficiency of body, yet you find him slovenly and unapt, then you shall trot him in some new plowed Field, soft and deep. But if he be of quick and of a fiery Spirit, apt, nimble and ready to learn, then you shall trot him in some sandy or gravelly place, where there is strong and firm foothold, and there you shall mark out a Spacious large Ring, at least threescore or fourscore paces in compass.

Having walked him six or seven times about the ring on your right hand, you shall then by a little tightening of your right Rein, and laying the Calf of your left Leg to his side, make a half

24

Circle within your Ring upon your right hand, down to the center or mid-point thereof, and then by tightening of your left Rein a little, and laying the Calf of your right Leg to his side, make another half circle to your left hand from the center to the outmost verge, which two half circles contrary turned will make a perfect figure eight within the Ring. Then keeping your first large circumference, walk your Horse about on your left hand, as oft as you did on your right, and then change within your Ring as you did before to your right hand again, and then trot him first on the right hand, then on the left, so long as you shall think convenient.

Although our ancient Masters in this Art have prescribed unto us certain numbers of Ring turns and how oft it is meet to go about on either hand, as if all Horses were of one even ability, yet I would wish you to neglect those Rules and only to practise your Horse in this Lesson according to the strength of his Body, more or less according to your discretion. For your change of hands, you shall do it as oft as shall seem best to your self, being ever very careful to give him the most exercise on whichever hand he is ever most unwilling to go. In this Lesson be careful also that he do it cheerfully, lustily, nimbly, quickening and inflaming his Spirits by all means possible.

Of Galloping large Rings.

When he will trot his Rings well, then in the same manner, and with the same changes, you shall make him gallop the same Rings, which he shall do also with great dexterity, lightness, and much nimbleness, without losing the least part or grace of his best Rein. Nay, so careful you shall be thereof that in his galloping, you shall as it were gather his Body together, and make his Rein rather better than it was, and make him take up his Feet so truly and loftily that not any Eye may see or perceive a falsehood in his stroke. His inward Feet should play before his outward, and each of a side follow the other so directly that his gallop may appear as the best grace of all his motions.

Neither shall you enter him into this Lesson rashly and hastily, but soberly and with discretion, making him first gallop a quarter of the Ring, then half, then three parts, and lastly the whole Ring. Neither shall you force him into his Ring with violence or with sharpness of Spurs, but with Spirit and Mettle, making him by the lightness and cheerfulness of your own Body, pass of his own accord into his gallop, and especially in his changes, where you may let him feel your Leg and show him your Rod on the contrary side. Herein is to be noted that continually those changes (in as much as they are made in a much tighter compass) must be done ever with great quickness and more stirring nimbleness than entire Lessons.

For the corrections in these large Rings, they be diverse, as namely, the *Bridle*, the *Spur*, and the *Rod*, and sometimes the *Voice*.

Corrections in the Ring-turns.

For the Bridle, you shall correct your Horse therewith if he carry his Head or Chaps awry or make ill-favored countenances, by giving now and then a little check in the Mouth and awaking him from such forgetful passions, or now and then drawing the bit to and fro in the Mouth, which will reform the error.

The Spur must be laid sharp and hard to his sides when you find your helps will do no good, but that his sloth rather more and more increaseth, or when he presseth and hangeth hard upon your hand or looseth the touch of his rein, or such like vices.

For the Rod, when you find that he neglecteth the showing or shaking of it, or when he disordereth any of his hinder parts and will not

gather them up comely together, then you shall therewith give him a sound lash or two under the Belly, or over the contrary Shoulder.

To any of these former Corrections you shall ever accompany the threatening of your Voice when the fault is too much foul and not otherwise, because there should be ever entire love betwixt Horse and Rider which continually chiding will either take away or at least root out the apprehension thereof.

Cherishings in his Ring-turns.

Now for your Cherishings, they are those which I formerly spake of, only they must be used at no time but when your Horse doth well and hath pleased your mind with his cunning and tractableness. Although the time for the same be when he hath finished his Lessons, yet there is a secret pleasing and cherishing of a Horse with the Bridle which must be exercised in the doing of his Lessons, and that is the sweetening of his mouth by a little easing of your Bridle hand and gently drawing it up back again, letting it come and go with such unperceiving motion that none but the beast may know it.

Of stopping and going back.

When your Horse can trot and gallop your large Rings with all perfectness, which with good industry will be perfected in less than a fortnight's

28

exercise, you shall then proceed to make him stop fair, comely, and without danger, which you shall do in the following manner.

First, as soon as you have taken his back, cherish him, put him gently forward, and bring him into a swift trot. After you have trotted him forty or threescore yards forward, you shall by drawing in your Bridle hand tightly and suddenly, make him gather his hinder Legs and fore-Legs together, and so in an instant stand still. As soon as he doth, immediately you shall ease your hand a little, but not so much as may give him liberty to press forward, but rather to yield backward, which if you find he doth, you shall give him more liberty and cherish him.

Having paused a while, draw in your Bridle-hand and make him go back two or three paces, at which if he strike, instantly ease your hand and draw it up again, letting him come and go till he yield and go backward, which (for the most part) all Horses at the first will do. If it be that your Horse rebel and will not go back with this gentle admonition, you shall then cause a Groom standing by to put him back with his hand, and in this motion you shall cherish him, that he may understand what your will is.

29

Helps.

Now for the helps in these Lessons, the best for stopping is the choice of ground. Make your Horse ever to stop down the slope of some hill or descending ground, whereby he may be compelled to couch the hinder loins the better and so stop most comely, and observe that the ground be firm and hard without danger of sliding, lest the Horse finding such an imperfection grow fearful and so refuse to do your will out of his own danger. In retiring you shall help him with your Rod, by putting it before his Breast or shaking it before his knees to make him remove his Feet more quickly and nimbly.

To ride for recreation.

If you intend to Ride only for Recreation, then you shall mark what Lesson your Horse is most imperfect in and with that lesson you shall ever when you ride both begin and end. After it, you shall fall to those lessons which are to your self most difficult and by the practice of them bring your self to a perfectness, then consequently to all other lessons, repeating (as it were) every one over more or less, lest want of use breed forgetfulness, and forgetfulness utter ignorance.

If your Recreation in Riding be tied to any special rules of health and that your practice therein proceed more from the Commandment

30

of your Physician than your pleasure, then I would wish you in the morning first to begin with a stirring or rough Lesson, which having a little stirred your blood and made it warm, you shall then calm it again with a gentler exercise. And thus stirring your blood with one lesson and with another moderately allaying such stirring, you shall give your body that due and proper exercise which is most fit for health and long life.

CHAPTER TWO

The Choice of the Horse for every several Use

For the choice of the best Horse, it is diverse, according to the use for which you will employ him.

If you would have a Horse for the Wars, you  *Horses for War.* shall choose him that is of a good tall stature, with a comely lean head, an out-swelling forehead, a large sparkling eye, the white whereof is covered with the eyebrows, and not at all discerned, or if at all, yet the least is best. A small thin ear short and pricking is preferable, but if it be long, well carried and ever moving is tolerable while if dull or hanging, most hateful. He should possess a deep neck, large crest, broad breast, bending ribs, broad and straight back, round and full buttock, with his hip bones hid, a tail high and broad, set neither too thick or too thin, for too much hair shows sloth and too little too much choler and heat. Also to be desired are a full-swelling thigh, a broad, flat, and lean leg, short

33

pasterned, strong jointed, and hollow bones, of which the long is best, if they be not weird, and the broad round the worst.

The best colors are brown-bay, Dapple-gray, Roan, bright-bay, Black, with a white near foot behind and a white far foot in front, white streak or white star, Chestnut or Sorrel, with any of these marks, or Dun with a black stripe. And of these Horses for the Wars, the Courser of *Naples* is accounted the best, then the *German*, the *Sardinian*, or the *French*.

Horses for a Prince's Seat.

If you would choose a horse for a Prince's Seat, any supreme Magistrate, or for any great Lady of State or woman of eminence, you shall choose him that is of the finest shape, the best rein, who naturally bears his head in the best place, without the help of the rider's hand; that is of nimblest and easiest pace, gentle to get upon, bold without making affrights, and most familiar and quiet in the company of other Horses. His color would ever be milk white, with red marks, or without, or else fair dapple gray with white Mane and white Tail. And of these the *English* is best, then the *Hungarian*, the *Swedish*, the *Polish*, the *Irish*.

Horses for Travel.

If you will choose a Horse only for travel, ever the better shape the better hope. Especially look

34

that his head be lean, eyes swelling outward, his neck well risen and his joints very strong. Let him be of a temperate nature, neither too furious, nor too dull, willing to go without forcing, and not desirous to run when there is no occasion.

Hunting Horses.

If you would choose a Horse for hunting, let his shape in general be strong, and well knit together, making equal proportions, for as unequal shapes show weakness, so equal members assure strength and endurance. Your unequal shapes are a great head to a little neck, a big body to a thin buttock, a large limb to a little foot, or any of these contraries, or where any member suits not with the whole proportion of the body, or with any limb next adjoining. Above all, let your hunting Horse have a large, lean head, wide nostrils, open jaw, a big throat, and the windpipe straight, loose, well-covered, and not bent in the pride of his Reining. The English Horse, bastardized with any of the former Races first spoke of, is of all the best.

Running Horses.

If you choose a Horse for running, let him have all the finest shape that may be, but above all things, let him be nimble, quick, and fiery, apt to fly with the least motion. Long shapes are sufferable, for though they show weakness, yet they assure sudden speed. And the best Horse for this use is the *Arabian*, *Barbary*, or his bastard; *Jennets* are good, but the *Turks* are better.

Coach Horses.

If you will choose a Horse for the Coach, which is called the swift draught, let his shape be tall, broad, and well furnished, not gross with much flesh but with the bigness of his bones. Especially look if he have a strong neck, a broad breast, a large back, sound clean limbs, and rough hooves; and for this purpose, your large English Geldings are best, your Flemish Mares next, and your strong Flemish Gelded Horses tolerable.

Pack-horses.

If you will choose a Horse for Portage, that is for the Pack or Hampers, choose him that is exceeding strong of Body and Limbs, but not tall, with a broad back, out ribs, full shoulders and thick withers, for if he be thin in that part, you shall hardly keep his back from galling. Be sure that he take a strong stride with his feet, for their pace being neither trot nor amble, but only a foot pace, he which takes the largest strides goes at the most ease and rides his ground fastest.

Cart-horses.

Lastly, if you will choose a Horse for the Cart or Plow, which is the slow draught, choose him of the most ordinary height, for Horses in the Cart unequally sorted, never draw at ease, but the

36

tall hang up the low Horse. Let them be of good strong portion, big breasted, large bodied, and strong limbed, by nature rather inclined to crave the whip, than to draw more than is needful.

For this purpose Mares are most profitable, for besides the effecting of your work, they yearly bring forth increase. If you furnish your draught with Mares to breed, observe in this wise to have them fair-fore-handed, that is, good neck, breast, and shoulders, for the rest is not so regardful, only let her body be large, for the bigger room a Foal hath in the dam's belly, the fairer are his members. And above all things, observe never to put your draught beasts to the Saddle, for that alters their pace and hurts them in their labors.

CHAPTER THREE

Ordering of the Horse

For the Horse for service, during the time of his teaching, which is out of the Wars, you shall keep him high and lustily, his food not Straw but good Hay, his provender clean dry Oats or two parts Oats and one part Beans or Peas, well dried and hard, the quantity of four quarts at watering, morning, noon, and evening is sufficient.

Ordering of Horses for War.

In his days of rest, you shall groom him betwixt five and six in the morning, water at seven, and feed at nine. In the afternoon, you shall groom betwixt three and four, water at four, and feed at six and again at eight. The night before he is ridden, take away his hay from him and at four in the morning give him a handful of Oats, then turn him upon his snaffle bit, rub all his body and legs over with dry cloths, and saddle him and make him fit for his exercise.

Soon as he is called for to be ridden, wash his bit in fair water and put it into his mouth with

39

all other things necessary, draw up his girths, see that no buckles hurt him, and then lead him forth. As soon as he hath been ridden, all sweating as he is, lead him into the stable, rub him quickly over with dry cloths, put on his housing-cloth, then set on the Saddle again and girt it. Lead him forth and walk him up and down in gentle manner an hour or more, till he be cold. After two or three hours fasting, turn him to his feed, and in the afternoon, curb, rub, and groom him, then water him and order him as is aforesaid.

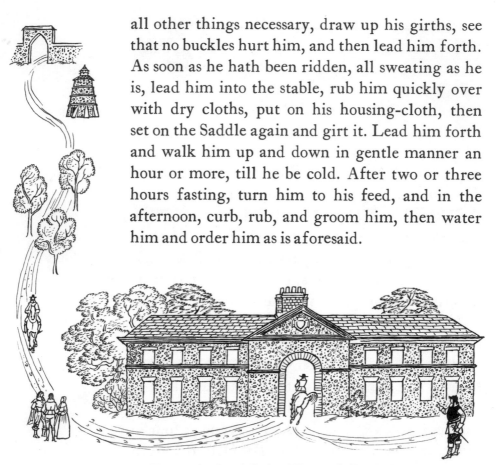

Ordering of Horses for a Prince's Seat.

For ordering of the Horse for a Prince, or great Lady's seat, let it be in his time of rest like unto the Horse for Service; and in his time of labor like the travelling horse, as shall be shown instantly: only because he is to be more choicely kept, I mean in the beautifullest manner, his coat lying smooth and shining, and his whole body without any stain or ill odors.

You shall ever when he hath ridden and cometh in much sweating, presently have him into the Stable, and first rub him down with clean wisps. Then taking off his Saddle, with a Sword-blade whose edge is dulled, you shall stroke his neck and body clean over, leaving no sweat nor filth than can be gotten out, then clothe him up, set on the Saddle, and walk him forth as aforesaid.

After, order and diet him as you do other travelling Horses: dry Oats is his best Provender if he be fat and full, and Oats and Beans if he be poor or subject to lose his flesh quickly.

For your travelling Horse, you shall feed him with the finest Hay in Winter, and the sweetest grass in Summer. His Provender will be dry Oats, Beans, Peas or bread, according to his stomach. In the time of rest, four quarts at a watering is sufficient; in the time of his labor, as much as he will eat with a good stomach.

Ordering of travelling horses.

When you travel, water him two hours before you ride, and then rub, groom, and lastly feed, bridle him up, and let him stand an hour before you take his back. Travel moderately in the morn-

41

ing till his wind be gotten and his limbs warmed, then after do as your affairs require. Give no feed whilst the outward parts of your horse are hot or wet with sweat, as the ear-roots, the flanks, the neck, or under his chaps, but being dry, rub and feed him according to the goodness of his stomach. Look well to his back, that the saddle hurt not, to the girths that they gall not, and to his shoes that they be large, fast and easy.

Ordering of hunting horses.

For the ordering of your Hunting-Horse, let him in the time of his rest have all the quietness that may be, much litter, much feed, and much dressings, water ever by him, and leave him to sleep as long as he pleaseth. Keep him to dung rather soft than hard, and look that it be well colored and bright, for darkness shows grease and redness inward heating. After exercises, let mashes of sweet malt be his usual purgings, and let bread of clean beans or beans and wheat equal mixt be his best food, and beans and oats the most ordinary.

Now for the hours of his feeding, it shall be in the morning after his coming from water, an hour after high-noon after his coming from his evening-water, and at nine or ten of the clock at night upon the days of his rest, but upon the days of his exercise, two hours after he is thoroughly cold inwardly and outwardly.

Lastly, for the preparation of food, you shall keep no certain quantity, but according to the horse's stomach, that is to say, you shall feed him by a little at once so long as he eats with a good appetite, but when he begins to trifle or fumble with his feed then to give him no more. Now for his Hay, you shall see that it be dry, short, uplandish hay, and so it be sweet, respect not how coarse or rough it is, since it is more to scour his Teeth and cool his Stomach than for nourishment expected from it.

For the ordering of your running Horse, let him have no more feed than to suffice nature, drink one in four and twenty hours, and grooming every day once at Noon only. Let him have much moderate exercise, as Morning and Evening Airings, or the fetching of his water, and know no violence but in his courses only. Let him stand dark and warm, have many clothes, and much litter, being

Ordering of running horses.

43

wheat straw only. If he be very fat, purge oft; if of reasonable state, purge seldom; if lean, then purge but with a sweet mash only.

Be sure your horse be empty before he courses, and let his food be the finest, lightest, and quickest of digestion that may be. The sweats are more wholesome that are given abroad, and the cooling most natural which is given before he come into the Stable.

Keep his limbs with cool ointments, and by no means let any hot spices come into his body. If he grow dry inwardly, washed feed is very wholesome. If he grow loose, then give him straw in more abundance. Burning of sweet perfume in the stable is wholesome, and anything you can either do about your horse, or give unto your horse, the more neat, cleanly, and sweet it is, the better it nourisheth.

Ordering of coach horses. For ordering the Coach horse, let him have good dressing twice a day, Hay and Provender his belly full, and Litter enough to tumble on, and he cannot choose but prosper. Their best food is sweet Hay and well dried Beans and Oats or Bean-bread.

Let him be walked and washed after travel, for by reason of their many occasions to stand still,

44

they must be inured to all hardness, though it be much unwholesome. Look well to the strength of their shoes and the galling of their harness. Keep their legs clean, especially about the hinder feetlocks, and when they are in the house, let them stand warm clothed.

For the ordering of the Pack-horse, or the Carthorse, they need no washing, walking, or hours of fasting. Only groom them well, look to their shoes and backs, and then fill their bellies, and they will do their labor. The best food is sweet Hay, Chaff, or Peas, or Oat-hulls and Peas, or chopped Straw and Peas mixt together. Once a week to give them warm Grains and Salt is not amiss.

Ordering of pack-and cart-horses.

Use oft to perfume his head with Frankincense, and in the heat of Summer use oft to swim him. Let a fat Horse drink oft, and a little at once, and a lean Horse whensoever he hath appetite. Much rubbing is comfortable and cheereth every member. Be sure to let your Horse eat grass once in a year, for that cooleth the blood, purges away gross humors, and gives great strength and nourishment to the body.

For the preservation of all Horses.

CHAPTER FOUR

Of Horses for Hunting

S ome love hunting for the exercise of their own bodies, some for the Chase they hunt, some for the running of the Hounds, and some for the training of their horses, whereby they may find the excellency of their goodness and endurance. To him therefore which placeth his delight in the goodness of his Horse, I would wish him to order and diet him, and he shall most assuredly come to the true knowledge of the best worth which is within him.

To ride in the Hunt.

A Hunting-horse would be groomed in his days of rest twice a day, that is, before he go to his morning watering and before he go to his evening watering. For the manner of his grooming after he is unclothed, you shall first curry him from the tips of the ear to the settling on of his tail, all his whole body most entirely over with an Iron comb, his legs under the knees and hocks only excepted. Then you shall dust him, then curry him again all

Grooming the Horse.

47

over with a round Brush of bristles, then dust him the second time, then rub all the loose hairs away with your hands wet in clean water, and so rub till the horse be as dry as at the first, then rub all his body and limbs over with a hair cloth. Lastly, rub him over with a fine white linen Rubber and pick his feet very clean. Clothe him and stop him round with wisps if you water within the house, otherwise saddle him after his body is wrapt about in a Woolen cloth and so ride him forth to the water.

*Watering
the Horse.*

The best water for a Hunting-horse is either a running River or a clear Spring remote from the Stable a mile or a mile and a half at most. As soon as you bring your horse to the water, let him drink, then gallop and leap him up and down a little, and so bring him to the water again and let him drink what he please. Having leaped him a little, walk him with all gentleness home, and there clothe him, stop him round with great soft wisps, and so let him stand an hour upon his bridle and then feed him.

*Clothing
the Horse.*

You shall clothe the Hunting-horse with a single cloth whilst the summer heat endureth, and after with more as you shall see occasion require. Now for as much as it is a rule with ignorant Riders that if they have but the name of keeping

48

a Hunting-horse they will with all care (without any reason) lay many cloths upon him, as if it were a special Physick, you shall know they are much deceived therein and may sooner do hurt than good with multiplicity of cloths. To clothe a Horse right, clothe according to the weather and the temper of his body, and thus if you see your Horse be slight, smooth, and well colored, then clothe him temperately, as with a single cloth of canvass or Sack-cloth at the most. If then as the year grows colder you find his hair rise and stare about his neck, flanks, or outward parts, then you shall add a woolen cloth, or more if need require, till his hair fall smooth again.

Touching the horse's exercise, which is only in the following of the hounds, you shall be sure to train him after those which are most swift and speedy; for so you shall know the truth and not be deceived in your opinion. Touching the days, it shall be twice a week at least but most commonly thrice.

Exercising the Horse.

CHAPTER FIVE

Of Horses for Travel

The Horse-rider whose occupation is in the general affairs of the Common-wealth, as some to the market, some to the City, and some to the seats of Justice, must necessarily be employed almost in continual travel, and therefore it is meet that he be provided ever of a good and easy travelling horse.

The marks whereby he shall choose a good travelling horse are these: he shall be of a good color and shape, lean headed and round fore-headed, a full eye, open nostril, wide jawed, loose throated, deep necked, thin crested, broad breast, flat chinned, out ribbed, clean limbed, short jointed, strong hoofed, well mettled, neither fiery nor craving, strong in every member, and easy to mount and get up upon. He shall follow without tugging and stand still when he is restrained.

The marks of a good travelling Horse.

If you travel, feed your horse early that he may take his rest soon.

General Rules for a travelling Horse.

51

In travel, by no means wash nor walk your horse but be sure to rub him clean.

Water him a mile before you come to your Inn or more as shall lie in your journey, or if you fail thereof, forbear it till next morning, for water hath often done hurt, want of water never did any.

Let your horse neither eat nor drink when he is extreme hot for both are unwholesome.

When the days are extreme hot, labor your horse morning and evening and forbear high-noon.

Take not your Saddle off suddenly but at leisure, and laying on the cloth, lay on the Saddle again till he be cold.

Litter your horse deep, and in the days of his rest let it also lie under him.

Groom your horse twice a day when he rests and once when he travels.

If the horse be gelded let him go to the soil and be purged with grass in May. A month's time

is long enough, and that grass which grows in Orchards under Trees is best.

In your journeying alight at every steep hill, for it is a great refreshing and comfort to your horse.

Before you sleep every night in your journey see all your horse's feet stopt with Ox-dung, for it taketh away the heat of travel and bruising.

Many other necessary Rules there are, but so depending upon these already showed that who so keepeth them shall not be ignorant of any of the rest, for they differ more in name than nature.

CHAPTER SIX

Of the breeding of all sorts of Horses

Our minds being swayed with many various motions, take delight sometimes to be recreated rather with contemplative delight than with active pleasures, and there is strong reason therefore. Disability of body or affairs of the Kingdom or Common-wealth may take a person from those preoccupations which otherwise might stir him to more laborious exercise, and of these contemplative Recreations I can prefer none before that gentle and beneficial delight of breeding creatures meet for the use of man and the good of the Common-wealth wherein he liveth. Of these breedings I cannot esteem any so excellent as the breeding of Horses, both for the pleasure we gain thereby in our own particular service and also for our strength, defence, and tillage of the kingdom.

He therefore that suiteth his recreation to the breeding of horses must first have respect unto the ground whereon he liveth or enjoyeth, for every ground is not meet to breed on, but some too good, some too bad. Some too good because they may be exhausted to a more beneficial commodity, Horses having a world of casualties attending on them and many years before the true profit arises. Some too bad because the extreme barrenness of the same will deny competent nourishment to the thing bred and so to the loss of time and profit add mortality.

Grounds to breed on. The grounds then meet to breed horses on would neither be extreme fruitful nor extreme barren, but of an indifferent mixture, yield rather a short sweet burden than a long, rich, and fruitful. It would rather lie high than low, but howsoever firm and hard under the foot. It would be full of Mole hills, uneven treadings, hills, and much cragginess, to bring Colts to nimbleness of foot, it would have good store of fresh waters, an open sharp air, and some convenient cover. This ground is best if it be several and enclosed.

Division of grounds. If you have much ground to breed upon, you shall divide it into many pastures, the least and barrennest for your Stallion to run with your Mares in, those which have least danger of waters are for your Mares to foal in, the fruitfullest and

56

of best growth, for your Mares to give milk in, and the most spacious and unevenest to bring up your Colts in after they are weaned.

For the choice of a good Stallion and which is best for our Kingdom, opinion swayeth so far that I can hardly give well-received Directions. Yet surely if you will be ruled by the truth of experience, the best Stallion to beget horses for the Wars is the *Courser*, the *Jennet*, or the *Turks;* the best for coursing and running is the *Barbary;* the best for hunting is the *Bastard Courser* begot of the *English;* the best for the Coach is the *Flemish;* the best for travel or burden is the *English;* and the best for ease is the *Irish hobby.*

For the choice of *Mares*, you shall greatly respect their shapes and mettles, especially that they be beautifully fore-handed, for they give much goodness to their Foals. For their Kinds, any of the *Races* before spoken of is very good, or any of them mixt with our true *English Races*, as *Bastard-courser Mare, Bastard-Jennet, Bastard-Turk, Barbary,* etc.

The best time to put your Stallion and Mares together is in the middle of March if you have any grass, as you should have great care for that purpose. One foal falling in March is worth two

57

falling in May, because he possesseth as it were two winters in a year and is thereby so hardened that nothing can (almost) after impair him. The best time to take your Horse from the Mares again is at the end of April or middle of May, in which you shall note that from the middle of March till the midst of May you may at any time put your Stallions to your Mares, and a month's continuance is ever sufficient.

Of covering Mares. For covering of Mares, it is to be done two ways, out of hand or in hand. Out of hand is when the Horse and Mares run together abroad, as is beforesaid, or turned loose into some empty barn for three nights one after another, which is the surest and the fastest way for a Mare's holding. In hand, early in a morning and late at an evening two or three days together, you bring the Horse to the Mare and make him cover her once or twice at a time holding him fast in your hand,

and when the act is done, lead him back to the stable.

To know if a Mare hold. To know whether your Mare hold to the Horse or no, there be diverse ways, of which the best is by offering her the Horse again at the next increase of the Moon, which if she willingly receive, it is a sign she held not before, but if she refuse, then it is most certain she is sped.

To provoke lust. If you have any advantage given you by friendship or otherwise whereby you may have a Mare at the present very well covered, only yours is not yet ready for the horse, you shall in this case to provoke lust in her, give her to drink good store of clarified honey and new milk mixt together, and then with a brush of nettles all to nettle her privy parts and then immediately offer her to the Horse.

To keep Mares from barrenness. To keep your Mares from barrenness and to make them ever apt to conceive foals, you shall by no means feed too extreme fat but keep them in a middle state of body by moderate labor, for the leaner they are when they come to take Horse, the much better they will conceive.

Ordering of Mares. After your Mares have been covered and that you perceive in them the marks of conceiving, you shall let them rest three weeks or a month

that the substance may knit. Then after, moderately labor or travel them till you see them spring,
and then turn them abroad and let them run till
they foal, for to house them after is dangerous
and unwholesome.

As soon as your Mare hath foaled, you shall
remove her into the best grass you have, which is
fresh and unsoiled, to make her milk spring. If
it be early in the year, you shall have a care that
there be good shelter in the same, and there let
her nourish her foal most part of the summer
following.

Weaning of Foals. As touching the weaning of foals, though some use to wean them at Michaelmas (September 29) or Martinmas (November 11) following, out of a supposition that the winter milk is not good or wholesome, yet they are much deceived. If you can by any convenient means (saving great losses), let your foals run with their Dams the whole year, even till they foal again, for it will keep the foal better in health, in more lust, and least subject to tenderness.

Ordering after the weaning. When you intend to wean your foals, you shall take them from their Dams over-night and drive them into some empty house where they may rest and the Mares be free from their noises. On

the morning following give to every foal fasting
a branch or two of Savin anointed or rolled in
butter, and then having fasted two hours after,
give him a little feed, as grass, hay, or Corn, with
some clear water, and do this three days together.

Seeing that they have forgotten their Dams,
geld such Colt-foals as you intend to make geldings of, and after their swellings are past, put
them and your other Colt-foals into a pasture
provided for them by themselves, and your Filly-
foals into another by themselves, which Pastures
may either be high woods, Commons, or such like
spacious pieces of ground where they may run till
they be ready for the Saddle.

CHAPTER SEVEN

The Art of Riding

Now forasmuch as to the Art of Riding belongeth diverse Turnings and Leaps right pleasant and curious to behold, and though not generally used in the Wars, yet not utterly useless for the same and many times very needful for the health of one's Body, I will by no means abridge our Perfect Horse-Rider of the same, but will proceed to the Lessons which are meet for Horses of pleasure.

When your Horse can stop and retire well, which may be done in the same space that you teach him his large Ring turns, you shall then teach him to advance before when he stoppeth, which is very comely and graceful to the beholders, and you shall do it in this manner. After you have stopped your horse, without giving your hand any ease you shall lay the Calves of both your Legs hard to his sides, and add thereto the noise of the shaking of your Rod, and your voice,

Of advancing before.

65

by crying *up, up,* which will at first (peradventure) but a little amaze him, because he understandeth not your meaning. Therefore you shall put him forward again and do as before, and that with a little more strength, continuing the practice of the same till you perceive he taketh one Foot from the earth, then cherish him a little. And so to the Lessons again, till he taketh up both his Legs from the ground, which when he doth, orderly or disorderly, yet cherish him exceedingly, that he may come to the knowledge of your meaning, without which all your labor is lost. Then to your former practice again, till you have brought him to that Perfectness that he will with all readiness advance as oft as you will give him the Calves of your Legs to his sides, be it less or more times together. This done, you shall look to the orderly and comeliness of his advancing, that he take up his Legs both even together, that he advance not too high (for fear of coming over upon you) but couch his hinder loins close to the ground, that he sprawleth not, nor paweth with his feet forward, and lastly that he advance not for his own pleasure, but when you command him by your own direct and orderly motions, for the contrary is a foul fault in Horse-riding.

66

For particular cherishings in this Lesson, they *Cherishings.* are no other than those former spoke of, only they must be done with a most ready watchfulness in the very instant and moment of time in which he performeth anything well, that the Horse may understand why and wherefore he receiveth such contentment and thereby be encouraged to continue in his goodness and be more ready to apprehend his rider's pleasure.

For the use of advancing, it is twofold; as *The use of advancing.* namely to give a grace to his other Lessons and to bring his body to nimbleness. Also it maketh a Horse apt and ready to turn well, and maketh him trust to his hinder Legs, whereby his fore-parts may be directed and governed at the Rider's pleasure.

Next to advancing, you shall teach your Horse *Of jerking behind.*

67

to jerk behind, in this manner: when at any time you have made him stop, you shall presently with your Rod give him a good jerk under the Belly near to his flank, which though at the first he apprehend not, yet by continual and constant use thereof you shall in the end bring him to jerk out his hinder Legs. At the first doing whereof, you shall cherish him, for that is the only language by which he knoweth he doth your will. Then having paused a little, make him do it again, increasing it every day and doubling his doings till he be so ready, that when you please to give the jerk, he will then give the jerk, and then you shall look to the comeliness of his doings.

Of turnings. When your Horse is perfect in the Lessons formerly spoke of, you shall then teach him to turn readily on both hands by narrowing his large Rings and bringing them into a much less compass. Although in the Art of Horse-riding there are diverse and sundry turns, some close and near the ground, as the turn *Terra, Terra,* or those we call *Carragolo, Serpeigiare,* and such like, and some swift and flying, as the *Incavallare, Chambetta,* and such like, yet they all labor but to one end, which is to bring the Horse to an exact swiftness and readiness in turning.

68

You shall make out a Ring some three or four yards in compass, coveting rather to tighten it than enlarge it, and you shall trot the Horse about the Ring first on the one side and then on the other, making your changes within that strait Ring as you did before within the large Ring. In this way, you teach him perfectly three Lessons together, that is the turn, *Terra, Terra*, the *Incavallare* and the *Chambetta*: the turn *Terra, Terra*, in the outmost circle of the narrow Ring, and the *Incavallare* and *Chambetta* in the changes, wherein he is forced to lap one leg over another, or else to lift up the inmost leg from the ground while he brings the outmost over it. Surely in this Ring and these changes consisteth the main art of

turning, and the chiefest glory both of Horse and Rider.

Your Horse being brought to this perfection that he will perfectly tread his large Rings, stop, retire, advance before, jerk behind, and turn readily on either hand, you shall then take away his nose-band and bit, and instead thereof put upon his Head a gentle nose-band of two joints and three pieces with a chap-band underneath, which you shall buckle close, but not tight, and be sure that the nose-band lies upon the tender gristle of the Horse's Nose somewhat near to the upper part of his Nostrils. Then to the chap-band you shall fasten the Martingale, and lastly to the rings on each side the nose-band you shall fasten long divided reins more than a yard and a half in length a piece. Then into his mouth you shall put a sweet smooth Cannon bit, with a plain watering chain, the cheek being of a large size so it may arm a little above the point of his shoulder, and the curb shall be thick, round and large, hanging loosely upon his nether lip and enticing the Horse with his lip to play with the same.

Thus armed you shall take his back, and so trot him forth the first morning outright a mile or two in the high way, making him only feel and grow acquainted with the bit, and only making him now and then stop and retire, and gathering up his head in a due place, and fashioning his rein with all the beauty and comeliness that may be, making him perfect with this bit as you did with the other one, which is an easy labor in as much as the bit is a much better command and brings more comeliness to the Horse's motion.

Now for as much as the Art in turning Horses is of great difficulty and ought of all lessons to be most elaborate, I will speak a little further thereof and show you the practice of these present times for the best accomplishment of the same without stirring up evil motions in the Horse, whence Restiveness and other vile errors do grow. It is certain that every Horse naturally desireth neither offence nor to offend, but the rash discretions of

Of the turning Post.

71

ignorant Riders, which will compel a Horse to do before he know what or how to do, is the begetting of those evils which are hardly or ever reclaimed. A Horse is like an ill brought up child, who having learnt drunkenness in his youth will hardly be sober in his age, and having once got a knavish quality, though he be never so much punished for the same, will yet now and then show that the remembrance is not utterly extinguished.

To prevent all those evils you shall cause a smooth strong Post to be well rammed and fixed in the earth in the midst of the narrow Ring at the very point and center thereof. Then causing a Groom to stand at the Post, you shall give him the right rein of your nose-band, which you shall make him hold about the Post, and so walk or trot your horse about the same on your right hand as long as you please. Then taking up the right Rein, give him up the left Rein and do as much upon the left hand, and thus change from hand to hand as oft as you shall think convenient, till you have brought your horse to the absolute perfection of every turn, the Post being such a guide and bound unto the horse, that albeit the rider were of him self utterly ignorant, yet it is impossible the horse should either disorder or disobey his purpose.

There is also another motion which is pleasing to the eye though it be very laborsome to the body, which is to make a Horse go side-long of which hand soever the Rider is disposed, and is very necessary in the Wars, because it is the avoiding of any blow coming from the Enemy. *Of going aside.*

When you intend to teach your Horse this motion, you shall draw up your bridle hand somewhat tight, and if you determine to have him go aside to your right hand, lay your left Rein close to his neck and the calf of your left leg close to his side, making him lap or put his left leg over his right. Then turning your Rod back-ward and jerking him gently on the left hinder thigh, make him bring his hinder parts to the Right side also, and stand in an even line as at the first. Then

73

make him remove his foreparts more than before so that he may stand as it were cross over the even line, and make him bring his hinder parts after and stand in an even line again.

Thus do till by long practice he will move his fore-parts and hinder parts both together and so side-long as far as you please, then cherish him, and if you will have him go towards your left hand, do as you did before, using all your helps and corrections on the right side only.

And thus much I think is sufficient to have spoke touching all the several Lessons meet to be taught to any Horse whatsoever, whether he be for service or for pleasure, and which being performed carefully and with patience, you may presume your Horse is Compleat and Perfect, the rather since no one can find out any invention or teach any other motion to a Horse which may be good and comely but you shall easily perceive that they are received from some one of these already rehearsed.

Now if you shall be called to Ride before a Prince, you must not observe the liberty of your own will, but the state of the person before whom you Ride and the grace of the horse which you ride. Coming into the riding place, you shall choose your ground so that the Person before whom you are to ride may stand in the midst thereof so as he may well behold the passage of the Horse to him and from him. Then being seated in a comely order and every ornament about you handsome and decent, you shall put your Horse gently forth into a comely trot.

Being come against the Person of state, bow your body down to the crest of your Horse, then raising your self again, pass half a score yards beyond him, and there marking out a narrow Ring, thrust your Horse into a gentle gallop and give him two or three turns in as short ground as may be to show his nimbleness and readiness. Upon the last turn, his face being toward the great person, stop him comely and close and make him to advance twice or thrice.

75

Then his face being towards the Prince, stop
him and give him fresh breath, then make him
jerk out behind, yet so as it may be perceived it
is your will and not the Horse's malice. Having
gone about the Ring and brought his face to look
upon the Prince, stop him again and give him
breath. Then drawing nearer to the Prince, you
shall beat the turn *Terra, Terra,* first in a pretty
large compass, then by small degrees narrowing
it to a little and a little, draw it to the very center,
where you may give two or three close flying
turns, and then changing your hands, undo all you
did before till you come to the Ring's first large-
ness. Having thus performed every motion orderly
and comely, bow down your body to the Prince,
and so depart.

THE Figure 1. a compleat *Horſeman* ſhows,
That *Rides*, *Keeps*, *Cures*, and all perfections knows.
The 2. *Diet* ; the 3. Letting Blood,
Beſt *Balm* of *Balms*, for inward Griefs moſt good :
The 4. *Wounds*, *Galls*, and *Sores* doth firmly cure ;
The 5. helps *Natures* Marks ; 6. doth procure
Helps for the *Sinews* Griefs, as *Slip* or *Strain*,
Knock, or *Convulſion*, all are helpt again.
The 7. wholſom *Drink* ; the 8. doth take
Blood from the *Mouth*, which ſudden Death doth ſlake.
The 9. ſhews the *Horſe-Caudle*, or the *Maſh*,
Good as the beſt, yet ſome Fools count it Traſh.
The 10. ſhews *Fury* in untamed things,
The only *Fountain* whence *Diſeaſes* ſprings.